A Painters' Place

Banks Head, Cumberland
1924 - 31

Abbot Hall Art Gallery
WITH
Redcliffe Press

Foreword

The inspiration behind this exhibition stems from a fascinating lecture on Winifred Nicholson delivered by her neighbour and fellow artist, Donald Wilkinson, to the Friends of Abbot Hall in 1982.

Donald Wilkinson spoke of the influence of the Cumberland scenery on the work of Ben and Winifred Nicholson during the years that they spent together at Banks Head, and illustrated how this artistic idyll was also enjoyed by Ivon Hitchens, Paul Nash and Christopher Wood. This community of artists talked, theorised and painted together, cross fertilising ideas and influencing techniques and approaches. Banks Head was an important artistic melting pot: this exhibition aims to draw attention to this hitherto over-looked aspect of the development of English painting in the 20th century.

We should especially like to thank Jake Nicholson and Judith Collins who have contributed a great deal of time and effort both to the research and the presentation of the material in the show and whose ideas and promptings have made a significant contribution to the overall direction of the exhibition and this publication. Particular thanks are also due to Donald Wilkinson for use of his photographs interpreting the painting sites and for his contribution to the overall direction of the project, to Peter Khoroche for invaluable help in locating many of Ivon Hitchens' paintings and to Angela Verren-Taunt for permission to reproduce examples of painting by Ben Nicholson. Without them this project would not have been possible. We should also like to thank James Austin who went far beyond the call of duty in photographing the paintings for reproduction.

Thanks are due to two other groups of enablers. The Lake District Art Gallery and Museum Trust wishes to record its gratitude to the Henry Moore Foundation and to Northern Arts for supporting this catalogue financially. We should also like to record our thanks to all the lenders of the paintings and drawings in the exhibition. Works have come from both private and public collections and we are grateful to all owners, whether individually acknowledged or anonymous, who have parted with their treasures for the duration of the tour.

The loans, exhibition tour and catalogue have been arranged and coordinated by Christian Barnes, Exhibitions Officer at Abbot Hall Art Gallery, to whom a final word of thanks is due.

It has been a great pleasure to have seen, and to present the paintings associated with Banks Head. We hope that visitors to the exhibition and those who read what follows will share in that enjoyment.

V. A. J. Slowe, Director, Abbot Hall Art Gallery & Museums, Kendal, Cumbria.

August 1991

Contents

Exhibition organised by Abbot Hall Art Gallery & Museums, Kendal, Cumbria.

This publication first produced for Abbot Hall Art Gallery in 1991
by Redcliffe Press Ltd, 49 Park Street, Bristol 1.

Judith Collins quotes from *Unknown Colour; Paintings, Letters, Writings*
by Winifred Nicholson, Faber & Faber.

ISBN 1 872971 46 6

Cover illustration: Kingwater Valley, Ben Nicholson: catalogue no. 26.

Typeset and printed in Great Britain by Taylor Brothers Bristol Ltd.

Banks Head – A Painters' Place

JUDITH COLLINS

In the early 1920s Winifred Nicholson's parents lived in a complex of houses at Boothby, outside the village of Brampton in Cumbria. From that base she and her husband Ben looked for a Cumbrian home of their own, and in the winter of 1923 they found Banks Head, an old stone farmhouse built over the remains of a Roman mile-castle on Hadrian's Wall, the border between England and Scotland.

Winifred described it as "a grey farmstead, a little house built out of the Roman Wall stones, a byre and a barn, on the line of the Roman Wall overlooking the great valley of the Irthing river, and over towards the blue-grey fells. It was to be sold with a few fields falling down to the river. It welcomed us and we bought it at once. The earth of Cumberland is my earth, way back to the Medieval, to the Roman times, the Celtic bronze-age times. I have always lived in Cumberland – the call of the curlew is my call, the tremble of the harebell is my tremble of life, the blue mists of lonely fells is my mystery, and the silver gleam when the sun does come out is my pathway."

Winifred's family had, from the sixteenth century, owned tracts of land and two castles – Naworth and Dacre – in North Cumberland so the country-side around Banks Head had a very strong ancestral and romantic attachment for her.

Equally the attraction of Banks Head and its environs to two young artists at the beginning of their career was its simplicity and its wild and isolated situation in open country. Winifred writes of her enjoyment of the changeable weather conditions found at Banks Head: "There is glittering sunshine and limpid rain in the sky, the plaything of the wind, which rushes it about and leaves it in the end in the grass and shiny amongst the sheep's scabious and cow dung . . . The wind blows right through your body . . . I don't want anything at all for the simple reason that I have everything, or rather, which is the same thing, everything has me." Winifred obviously experienced a passionate identification with this parcel of Cumbrian earth and its climate, which began to insinuate itself in her paintings. She believed that Banks Head and its neighbouring borderlands also spoke to Ben in a similar way: "all the Scots ancestry of him came into play, the Scots stark simplicity, the order of the tartan square lines, the agility and the lilt of the sword dance and the reel."

Before Ben and Winifred moved into Banks Head, in the late spring of 1924, they asked the local builder to alter some of the windows to make them "squat and unsymmetrical with square squat window panes, as per the character of Banks Head." In all the houses in which the Nicholsons lived and worked, and most particularly at Banks Head, Winifred remembered that "one paid heed to the windows, their outlook, their curtains, the light to let in illumination." In a letter to Edith Jenkinson, a friend and fellow painter, Winifred wrote how she and Ben were looking forward to moving into Banks Head on May 1st 1924, even if they had to share it "with the Plumber, the Carpenter, the Cesspool maker and the Distemperer." Even before they moved in, Winifred began creating a garden from the sloping, wind-tossed land to the south of the house.

The Nicholson-designed windows set into the large front kitchen and bedrooms, with their large sills ready to accommodate vases of wild flowers from the garden, allowed scenic views looking south from the back of the house over to Cold Fell and Tindale Fell, the northern end of the Pennines (see cat. no.17). Winifred worked upstairs in a room at one end of the farmhouse which looked west across Banks Head farmyard while Ben "made a studio out of the barn, looking down the Roman Wall to the east and the Nine Nicks of Thirlwall."

Almost as soon as Banks Head was habitable (although it lacked electricity and water) in July 1924, Paul Nash and his wife Margaret were invited to stay, probably in return for the visit that Ben and Winifred had paid to the Nashes at Dymchurch on the Kent coast during the previous summer. And then in summer 1925, it was the turn of Ivon Hitchens, one of the founder members of the Seven and Five Society, a group of seven painters and five sculptors who first exhibited together in London in 1920 with no set programme as their aim. He was the only artist to last the full course of annual exhibitions until the Society's demise in 1935. In 1924 Hitchens introduced Ben Nicholson as a member, and in 1925 Ben brought Winifred into the Society. In 1926 Ben and Winifred proposed Christopher Wood as a member, and Ben was elected Chairman of the Society. With Hitchens initiating the introduction of the Nicholsons and they in turn bringing along Wood, the Seven and Five Society was from circa 1926 to 1932 the most avant-garde group among London artistic circles, with much of its artistic experimentation taking place in the working atmosphere of Banks Head. Paul Nash was the only Banks Head visitor not to join the Society.

Hitchens sent six works on average to each Seven and Five annual exhibition from 1920 to 1924. They were mainly depictions of the Sussex downs under different weather conditions and showed some influence from modern French painting, particularly Cézanne. Hitchens was learning to use the landscape as a vehicle for experimentation in terms of form and colour and this approach allied him to contemporary work by the Nicholsons.

In the summer of 1925 Ben and Winifred Nicholson invited Hitchens to paint with them at Banks Head. Hitchens stayed for two months in total, staying on alone after the Nicholsons had left for their rented flat in London. Of the seventeen oils which comprised Hitchens's first one-man show at the Mayor Gallery in December 1925, five interiors and two landscapes — A Border Day and A Cumberland Highway — would appear to be paintings executed at Banks Head or inspired by it. Hitchens had never attempted anything but landscapes until his visit to Banks Head, but obviously something about the quality of the farmhouse rooms inspired him to produce sensuous and rhythmic responses to this visual stimuli. Although Hitchens does not introduce any figures into his Banks Head interiors, there is always the implied presence of Ben and Winifred Nicholson because what Hitchens has chosen to paint is their domestic space with its idiosyncratic combinations of colour, textiles, furniture and objects. Hitchen's series of Banks Head interiors could be seen as a homage to his working friendship with the Nicholsons in Cumbria.

Not since the Mayor Gallery exhibition in 1925, a gap of sixty-six years, have Hitchens's paintings of Banks Head interiors been reassembled in such depth. This exhibition offers therefore a most valuable opportunity to assess them. The two paintings of the bedroom, especially The Green Table (cat. no.31), show Hitchens employing a new range of warm to hot colours often set down with patches of undulating brushmarks. In the two bedroom paintings Hitchens has made interesting use of the full-length mirror which leans at an angle against the wall to the right of the window. Like the view glimpsed through the window, the mirror and its reflection indicate a space larger than that of the somewhat cramped bedroom with its overlapping soft forms. The mirror frames an interior view while the window beside it frames an exterior view and this interplay between interior and exterior was one that had already entered the vocabulary of Winifred Nicholson's paintings from circa 1922, in the guise of flowers set in vases on window sills. Hitchens conjures an ambiguous sense of space in both Abstract

Interior (cat. no.30) and Cottage Interior (cat. no.32), two views of Banks Head front kitchen; the upright rectangle in Abstract Interior can be read as both a mirror and a door.

In the early 1920s Hitchens attempted to create space chiefly by the use of different spatial planes; by 1925 he had realised that colour equally has space creating properties. Creating space through colour was a programme that Winifred Nicholson followed with great success. She would plan a composition of a landscape or flowers on a window sill by preliminary pencil sketches, and then she would choose two or three strong and contrastingly vibrant colours from which to build a luminous picture. She wrote that she wished to paint pictures that "call down colour, so that a picture can be a lamp in one's home, not merely a window." She believed that colours were free, and not "nailed down" to forms and her conception of a painter was someone who caught colours while they were on the wing, as it were, on their journey from the sun, the source of all light and therefore all colour. In order to keep her chosen colours fresh, she painted fast and tried to finish a painting in one sitting. A characteristic and much employed brush mark in her work was that of a long rippled horizontal stroke, which perhaps echoed the waves of colour and light that transversed the atmosphere. It is just this brush mark that can be found entering Hitchens's painting from circa 1925, the time of his stay at Banks Head; Winifred had employed it since 1921-2 so the direction of the influence is obvious.

Winifred had painted landscapes in the open air from the time that she was a student at the Byam Shaw School of Art just prior to the First World War using a range of local, descriptive colours. When she moved to Banks Head she continued to work outside directly in front of her beloved Cumbrian motifs and employed a rich palette of greens, greys and browns. In The Swaites (cat. no. 10), one of her most accomplished early Cumbrian landscapes, both the distant sky and foreground fields are painted with the same choppy brushstrokes and the same weight of tonal values. A sense of deep perspectival space is created by the hedgerow borders of the central field converging on the white-washed farmhouse. To reinforce this, the scale of the animals in the field decreases. The same compositional device, path or hedgerow snaking back from the foreground to background to end at a farm building, is also found in Northrigg Hill (cat. no.11). This formula is abandoned in Landscape: Road along the Roman Wall (cat. no.9) because the silvery white colour of the road is the same as that found in the sky and neighbouring field.

Winifred has begun to eschew the creation of pictorial space through perspectival recession in favour of a harmonious relationship of high keyed colours boldly announcing their placement on the flat two-dimensional picture plane. Because the brushwork which described the forms is so loose and airy, the forms of the landscape begin to dissolve in the light. Winifred found her own special way of combining the near and the far – the wide expanses of illusory pictorial landscape space – by breaking up light and colour so that they become tossed to and fro within the composition "like a shuttlecock".

Winifred liked to paint in many different kinds of light, listing sunlight, moonlight, dawn and dusk, candlelight and snowlight as interesting possibilities. She had learned to work out in landscapes covered with snow when she and Ben lived for the first three years of their married life in a house, the Villa Capriccio, high above Lake Lugano in the Swiss alps, where snow covered the ground in the winter months. Villa Capriccio was sold in 1923 in favour of the attraction of a home in Cumbria; however the Border climate also offered its fair share of snowy landscapes for painting purposes, and Irthing Snow (cat. no.8) is a fine example of this genre. In complete contrast to the cold winter picture of Irthing Snow is Fire *and Water* (cat. no.12), a work which celebrates the warmth and colour of fire light, and the focal point of the front kitchen at Banks Head. Winifred used colour to create a mood and to establish the composition in her paintings, and this approach was shared by Christopher Wood. He met the Nicholsons in London in July 1926 and painted with them at St Ives in Cornwall from August to October. From that time on, letters between them indicate that the Nicholsons issued an open invitation for Wood to come and paint with them at Banks Head. He learnt from their words and from their paintings that the ambiance at Banks Head was most conducive to work, offering a close experience "of earth and of wind". Writing about Wood after his early death in 1930, Winifred noted that his paintings followed a progression in their use of colour; first there was blue with black, then a period of green, then blue with white. The period of green coincided with Wood's stay at Banks Head which lasted from March to April 1928, the point at which his mature style was formed. Winifred recounted the impact of his visit to Cumbria in March 1928: "His arrival was like a meteor. The wild country delighted him . . . We all three painted and thought of nothing else. Inspiration ran high and flew backwards and forwards from one to the other. Usually he painted from drawings or from memory, but here he painted some pictures from nature, carrying an enormous box of paints and easel over the rough fields and walking at his usual swift pace."

The inspiration of which Winifred wrote stemmed from the three artists' commitment to the same aims, the most prominent of which at that time was a type of primitivism. Since his death, Wood and his paintings have often been described as 'innocent' with an air of 'incorruptibility', and much the same words could have been used of Winifred too. Being an 'innocent', 'primitive' artist in 1928 meant rejecting academic conventions and simplifying technical and formal means. Ben Nicholson was well known for his rejection of bourgeois living, with its strict code of dress and manner. He was fond of quoting the phrase 'ginger biscuits' when a formal social occasion, sometimes connected with Winifred's family, threatened to overwhelm him.

Ben too wished to unlearn much that he had been taught at art school, and he began to produce paintings with a new sense of directness and simplicity. The directness and consequent immediacy stemmed largely from technical processes. Ben Nicholson had first begun to stress the substance and reality of the brushmarks which make up a painting in 1923 when he painted with Nash at Dymchurch. A primer layer of white paint was laid on roughly and thickly and the brushmarks of that layer showed through the later layers of coloured pigment. This insistence on the material qualities of the picture, on brushmarks loaded with paint, drew great attention to the flat two-dimensional quality of the picture's surface. In the mid-1920s Ben Nicholson worked towards the creation of a picture space that rejected traditional perspective. In *Birch Craig, Winter* (cat. no.18) and *Hare Hill* (cat. no.22), for example, odd patches of colour appear in the field areas and round the naively drawn animals. These patches of colour play their part in the evocation of a wintery landscape as well as announcing their presence as areas of pigment laid down with a brush.

Winifred recalled that in 1928 Christopher Wood had introduced her and Ben to a priming preparation called Coverine. It was a thick white paint which dried fast and "you can put it over old pictures". Recycling rejected paintings by this method was most obviously practical, but it also ensured that the second painting to be created on a canvas or board that already had the first attempt covered over with Coverine would ride above stratified layers of earlier painterly activity. These several layers of brushstrokes would add a sense of vivacity and animation to the new painting, which would enhance its directness and immediacy, and this can be found in many of the Banks Head paintings by Winifred and Christopher Wood in this exhibition. But equally the layers could function somewhat retrospectively, and give a sense of history to the new work. H. S. Ede, an art critic, wrote about the nature of the paintings produced by members of the Seven and Five Society in 1927, when it was a major exhibiting forum for the Nicholsons, Wood and Hitchens, and he used the phrase "beauty caught on the wing". Ben Nicholson refuted this description of his paintings at the time, and announced that his aim then was to make "something particularly primitive, sustained and enduring."

In the autumn of 1928 when the Nicholsons and Wood were painting together in St Ives, a place just as wild and windy and primitive as Banks Head, they discovered Alfred Wallis with his naive paintings and his unschooled, unspoilt eye. Winifred wrote of Wallis: "He paints all day – imaginative, elemental, strange paintings on scraps of cardboard or odd boxes. His simple ferocity makes most recognised painting look utterly insipid." This discovery of Wallis and his work came after the Nicholsons and Wood had ventured along the path of elemental simplicity when sharing ideas at Banks Head and it reinforced all they had learnt from one another at that time.

The heady, experimental years at Banks Head – 1924-31 – produced an excellent vintage which this exhibition celebrates. But by 1931 Christopher Wood was dead and Ben Nicholson was ready to move on to other pastures. Winifred, in her indomitable manner, lived and worked at Banks Head until her death in 1981 and made many more pictures which evoke "the call of the curlew" and "the tremble of the harebell" but that is another story.

What Does An Artist Look For In A Painting Place?

JAKE NICHOLSON

Why did Winifred and Ben Nicholson decide to settle in Cumberland when they returned from Italian Switzerland? The obvious reason was that Winifred's parents lived nearby and that this was where Winifred had spent part of her childhood. But was it also that the view from Banks Head, looking down over the river valley and up to the fells on the other side was similar to the view they had found so paintable in Lugano? In fact they tried to make the bleak Cumbrian farmhouse feel more like Switzerland by planting a walnut tree and almond trees. The surprising thing is that they grew! The walnut tree is still there – though stunted in growth.

What else does a painter look for? The view was constantly changing. One day, just before rain, the fells look so close you can almost touch them. Another time they will disappear in the mist so that you wouldn't know they were there at all. In winter the high fells can be covered with snow while the lower hills are brown or dull green. Each window of the house was like a picture frame holding the view beyond. The proportions and fenestration of the windows were carefully designed by Ben. The old stone walls made deep sills, on which jugs of flowers could stand and relate to the landscape.

Artists need space to think. Ben and Winifred chose studios at opposite ends of the house. Ben's was in what used to be the hay loft, with a view out to the East, and a tiny door to "keep visitors out".

I wonder if we realise how poor our lives have become now that so many of us are separated from our animals? Even in the country herds of dairy cows are more large and impersonal. Before the war Cumberland was one of the most advanced counties agriculturally – the first county to be TT tested. Each farm had at least one working horse, probably a Clydesdale. When not working they grazed in the fields – an easier way of refuelling than the "horsepower" of the tractor! Ben's landscapes often have a horse in at least one of the fields.

Although Winifred brought the girls from the Byam Shaw Art School from London to work as land-girls during the First World War, and was used to working and ploughing with horses, she tended to paint cows – as in *The Swaites,* or the dark cow-smelling picture of cow-byre in the farm next door. At Banks Head there was always the sound of cocks and hens scratching around in the farmyard. It's sad that, in so many places, this sound has been replaced by the roar of a battery hen-house.

One of our dogs was a Border Collie called Slinky, or Slinks, because he used to slink around to our own hen-house on the East side of Banks Head, and gently remove an egg in his mouth – going off to a corner where he crushed it, then ate the contents. There were always cats around at Banks Head, which Ben preferred to dogs. Also plenty of field and house mice which wintered in the old stone walls. Winifred forbade the maids to kill them, so they had to resort to protecting food by covering the food with bowls in 'Tailor of Gloucester' fashion.

The house was very simply furnished. All Victorian ornamentation was banished. The front kitchen had a large black range on one side of the room. It had an oven on the left, and a water heater on the right. Both worked with dampers from the central fire grate, on which a kettle or pan was always singing. Winifred painted this in a picture called *Fire and Water*. She wrote: "Banks Head's altar was its hearth".

There were rag rugs on the stone flagged floors. Mary Bewick (née Warwick), one of the daughters of the farmer next door, made rag rugs and Ben designed one for her to make up. It had fifteen twelve-inch squares, with an animal or bird in alternate squares – a horse, dog, turkey, cat, ram, black hen, white duck and a cock. Ben discarded the traditional form of floral border. In later years Winifred painted a picture on South Uist called *Cheeky Chicks,* where hens crept into the picture.

Ben and Winifred were not so interested in wild animals and birds at this stage, but Winifred was interested in wild flowers. In those days the road was a stone road – not tarmacked. It had wide verges full of cowslip, early purple orchid, ragged robin, harebell and other wild flowers. Winifred often gathered a bunch of these and brought them home to paint. Wild flowers and garden flowers, too, were subjects she shared with Christopher Wood. There is a painting of heartsease pansies by him. Although Ben painted flowers at this period, in his pictures the jug is always more important than the flowers. With Winifred and Christopher Wood it is the other way round. Though Ivon Hitchens loved foliage and bushes he painted interiors at Banks Head – but the colours he used make the paintings feel as if they were outside. Perhaps he simply didn't like carrying his paints around? Or was the weather too bad to go out?

Not surprisingly there were maids at Banks Head – one usually sleeping in, and the other coming in by day. Both Winifred and Ben had been used to help in the house before they were married, but it was also necessary for them to have help if they were both to continue painting. Amy Little, one of the maids at that time, still lives nearby. Winifred painted several portraits of Amy, emphasizing her flaming red hair. She says how much she enjoyed working at Banks Head as it was "a happy house". It was hard work, though, in an unmodernised house with no electricity and stone flagged floors. Winifred spent time after breakfast each morning giving the maids their tasks, and was quite firm. Ben had a more relaxed attitude and was always joking and pulling their legs.

Amy Little also likes to recall the row of smart ties which Ben kept hanging on a string behind his bedroom door – many with spots. She says how smart he always looked – though he did turn up at one of his mother-in-law's (Lady Cecilia's) garden parties in a red jumper in order to shock! There was nothing Bohemian in the way the house was run, or in the way that they dressed, nor in the attitude of their friends. Christopher Wood was quite dapper, often wearing a bow tie in the country!

In the early days at Banks Head, Ben and Winifred would carry their paints, canvases and drawing materials to a chosen painting site. As these were heavy, the distances were limited, so it was mostly the nearby farms which they painted. The same applied to Christopher Wood when he came. However, while Ben chose sites that you looked up to, Christopher Wood preferred to look down into the valleys. In time Ben acquired an Austin 7, so they were able to move around the countryside and choose places to draw and paint.

Ben loved cars, steam trains and aeroplanes. He introduced the train across the valley into his pictures. I remember as a small boy being hauled out of bed to see a huge airship sailing up the valley. Winifred never understood anything mechanical. Machines, however beautiful, never appeared in any of her pictures. Christopher Wood loved boats, and of course painted them – but there weren't any in East Cumberland.

Banks Head has been a place since Roman times; and a farm since the Borders were pacified: but it needed the eye of an artist to see it as a painters' place. Other artists then came and shared ideas, some of the first were those in this exhibition, and others came later in the inter-war years. Different artists came after the war; and more recently, to live and work in the surrounding area.

Do you have an internal antenna which will receive ideas as much in a prison or hospital as in a beauty spot? Or have you found a place where your creative ideas will flow?

11

Banks Head 'Front Kitchen' with black fireplace. Slinky lies asleep on the rag rug Ben is known to have designed and which was made by Mary Bewick.

Banks Head Recollections

DONALD WILKINSON

In her letters and conversation Winifred Nicholson often described particular locations as being good places in which to paint; or where she could paint and be happy. Banks Head was the place that Ben and Winifred found which became their shared painting place from 1924 until 1931. During this time and later, various friends were invited to come and paint or write and to share its solitude. Although she travelled a great deal – painting in all sorts of places – Banks Head was the centre of Winifred's creativity and remained throughout her life a 'Painters' place'.

It was late November in 1975, a changeable morning with trees bright against an indigo sky, a hawthorn glowing with berries and black Galloway cattle grazing in winter fields beyond.

As the car climbed the hill above the Priory we entered a different landscape. To our right we got glimpses of land falling away below with a pattern of small fields, woods and farms on the far side of the valley. In the distance the bulk of a fell loomed against a heavy sky.

This was one of our first visits to Banks Head. Banks Head is on the ridge which leads down into the river valley. When you approach, it looks like any other North Cumbrian farmhouse built of stone with stone slab roof, and its small windows facing north give very little away about the atmosphere of the interior. There are mature beech trees close to the house and grass rather than lawn below, which in spring is carpeted with snowdrops and crocus. In front, not seen until one enters the living room, there is a garden with shrub roses, all sorts of poppies and other old varieties of flowers. It has apple trees and a plum tree and is sheltered by beech and holly.

The Banks Head living room was full of light, with nicotianas and winter jasmine on the window-sill silhouetted against small rivers of rain.

As a rainbow shone over the stubble field, we walked before lunch through fir woods down into the river valley, views of the river appearing between trees, a golden river flowing swiftly in its gorge.

Over lunch, "What are the colours in a rainbow, and where do they come from?" Winifred asked our children. Still sitting at the table we looked at paintings as they were brought into the room and were asked to help to choose titles for ones recently finished – "Titles are so important". Later we were shown books, one by Burne-Jones was taken out of its blue-green leather case. Winifred questioned me about the illustrations, wondering if they were hand-coloured etchings.

We looked at other paintings and then went upstairs to see the views across the valley towards Tindale and the Lake District fells further away. This was a new landscape to us which seemed very peaceful, a landscape which appeared under various weathers in many of the paintings, in snow, at sunrise or in summer haze.

This was one of many days spent with Winifred enjoying her conversation, the atmosphere of Banks Head, and coming home filled with memories of her paintings.

I am reminded of another time from looking at a photograph I took one evening in 1979. It is of the table covered with a red checked cloth, a small hand-made pot holding a bunch of yellow pansies and purple primulas, and a series of paintings on paper are spread out for us to see. The paintings are ideas of shells against waves and arcs of rainbows in space. We discussed the colour and the combination of media – gouache, oil wash and oil pastel. The paintings were on heavy hand-made paper and ideas had developed from one sheet to the next.

We had been invited to supper, Winifred was on her own as Kate, her daughter, was away having an exhibition in Colchester. Although it was dark outside the curtains had been left undrawn so that we could enjoy the flowers on the window-sills. The room was full of flowers and paintings. Ben Nicholson's first relief was hanging above Winifred's chair, one of Winifred's snow paintings and another of irises and hyacinths were in the corner. On the stone wall was a painting she had made of Rhum from the Isle of Canna, in the Hebrides. Over the hearth, an abstract canvas by Kate, arabesques on the pristine white ground painted in St. Ives.

Winifred sat in her chair and we talked about painting and how it happens, how for her it was important to have an object or image as a starting point for her imagination to work. Winifred was pondering on the fact that although women poets and writers have been credited with masterpieces, no woman had yet been recognised as having painted a masterpiece, no woman had yet been thought of as a great painter. Later she took me round the house. In the bedroom was one of the paintings made by Christopher Wood from his stay in 1928. It was a sombre image of fields and woods, the fells snow-covered and the River Irthing flowing below. Of all the painters who came to stay and work at Banks Head his was the imagination that Winifred most admired. Ben and Winifred met many artists in London and through exhibiting with the Seven and Five. The artists they invited to stay were those with whose ideas they were in sympathy. Winifred remained interested in people and ideas throughout her life, not only about painting but about politics and religion.

During this period they were friendly with Ivon Hitchens and obviously all three shared a response to nature in their work. It was a time of mutual discovery

Christopher Wood, Winifred Nicholson and Jake—Cumberland, 1928

and looking at things with a fresh eye – many years later, in our various discussions about this period, Winifred never mentioned Hitchens or his work.

Winifred would often talk about Ben and his paintings and about working with him in Italian Switzerland and elsewhere – she admired his single-mindedness and his genius.

There were paintings and drawings at Banks Head from his many periods, from the early small Cumbrian landscapes with their white farms to reliefs and his only sculpture through to large abstracts with their subtle range of colour. Winifred would take me into the studio that had been Ben's and pull out drawings from the picture racks; I remember one called *Bre Ticino* made in 1921, and others unframed of farms and barns and animals in fields. I was told he drew each day because his father, the painter Sir William Nicholson, thought he would never make a painter if he could not draw.

One was reminded of the early days at Banks Head, the sharing of ideas and discoveries, Ben and Winifred working all day in their separate upstairs studios. After breakfast Winifred would discuss the menu and the household tasks for the day with the girls from the nearby farm and village who came to help, and then was not to be disturbed until lunchtime. Winifred's studio looked out towards the farm next door, into the yard and the gable-end of the farmhouse and beyond to the Roman signal station. Ben worked at the other end of the house with views looking east along the straight road bordered by dry stone walls and fields. Here and there a farm and its outbuildings are visible in a shelter of trees. The days were planned to make as much time for painting as possible, callers were to be discouraged before 4.30 p.m.; sometimes a note would be pinned to the outside door to this effect. Winifred's sister did call before this time, unannounced, found Ben walking in the garden and did not understand that this was part of the thinking process he used to sort out his ideas.

15

During this period they often walked and made drawings on the spot, sometimes from the same motif. They each drew Craig Hill dipping their pens in a shared bottle of Indian ink. Ben was considered fun and had an impish sense of humour. He was made welcome at the farms when he called. A farmer's daughter recalled a childhood memory of Ben coming and sitting cross-legged in front of the kitchen fire and joking with them all.

As we continued round the house, in her studio bedroom Winifred showed me her most recent group of paintings—her prismatic paintings, beautiful, enjoyable images, full of optimism, small glowing canvases, ideas of flowers and rainbows. They were leaning against the wall, on the chest and standing on chairs. Winifred wondered what people would make of them—they were important to her. Brushes and tubes of colour were spread out on the table between the windows ready for use. On the walls were other paintings, an unframed Ben Nicholson canvas in pale ochres and grey hung on a nail above the chest of drawers; on the chest a pile of sepia photographs; Victorian botanical studies were next to a delicate Indian miniature. We looked at catalogues, and I asked about David Jones. She said that he had given her a wood engraving, which was kept in a book. She also found the small book Paul Nash had given her—a copy of his *Places* of 1922, a book of wood engravings of landscape.

Paul Nash and his wife came to stay at Banks Head in the summer of 1924. I learned from Winifred that Nash had not found the landscape to his liking but had been excited by glimpses from the windows as the train climbed over Shap on the way to Carlisle. He made a number of drawings near the house of the large beech tree, including the end wall of the barn as part of the design. In the drawings the tree is called a walnut, but Winifred said it was a beech tree. The only walnut tree at Banks Head was the one that Ben and Winifred had recently planted, not a mature tree as shown in the drawing. Maybe he found the country here wilder than he was used to, not as lush as Oxfordshire or Wiltshire, or maybe he was feeling his way with this new landscape.

Their stay was cut short by a tragedy when Winifred's sister-in-law died in childbirth. Winifred said that they intended to come and stay again, but never did.

All the drawings that I have seen that Nash made on this visit were done near the house or from the garden looking towards the east or south with trees playing an important part in the composition.

On an autumn afternoon towards the end of Winifred's life I was up at Banks Head. She had been working all day—painting in her bedroom-studio upstairs. After I had had a cup of tea with her and Kate, she asked if I would like to come and look at what she had been doing. The painting was an idea based on the view from her window of the large beech trees seen against the pale violet of Tindale Fell—the remaining leaves on the trees are chrome orange.

The paint is laid on spontaneously, no fuss, the interior suggested by curtains and table-top beneath the window-sill. Winifred was not happy with the handling of the curtains so far. As we looked and talked, through the window overlooking the farmyard the sun was setting beyond the Solway, casting a golden glow over the whole landscape. At the same moment from the other window we watched the new moon rise over the fell. Winifred's question was: "Could you paint it?"

CHRISTOPHER WOOD

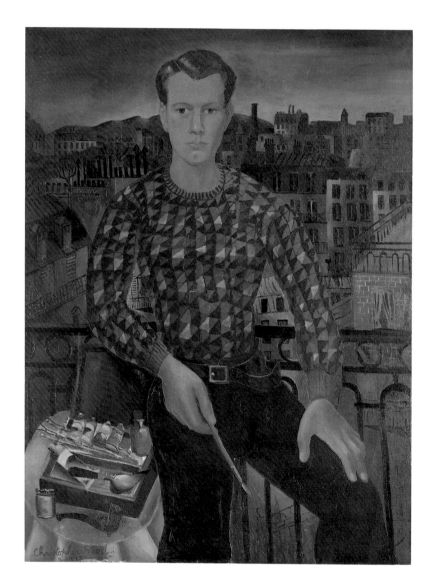

Self Portrait 1927 (Kettle's Yard)

Westmorland Landscape (Arts Council collection)

Banks Head, Cumberland 1928 (Rugby Borough Council on loan to the University of Warwick)

Cumberland Landscape 1928 (Manchester City Art Galleries)

WINIFRED NICHOLSON

The Swaites 1923

Northrigg Hill

Large Landscape with Two Houses (Landscape: Road along the Roman Wall)
(Kettle's Yard)

Irthing Snow (Mr and Mrs Andras Kalman)

Fire and Water 1927

Amy in the Kitchen at Banks Head 1929

Banks Head Flowers in an Alabaster Vase

BEN NICHOLSON

Birch Craig Winter 1930

Birch Craig Summer

Landscape with Haystacks 1928

Hare Hill 1930

Window at Banks Head (Fine Art Society)

Striped Jug and Flowers 1928

IVON HITCHENS

Cottage Interior 1925

Abstract Interior 1925 (Ivor Braka)

Cottage Bedroom 1925

The Window-Sill 1925

46

The Green Table 1925

The Bridge at Lanercost (Lake District Art Gallery & Museum Trust)

PAUL NASH

The Walnut Tree 1924 (Piccadilly Gallery)

CATALOGUE

Catalogue

The catalogue is organised into sections devoted to each artist. Entries list the title; the date (where known); medium; measurements in centimetres, height before width excluding frame; previous exhibitions (where known) are given in italics and lenders to the exhibition in brackets.

CHRISTOPHER WOOD

1. **Westmorland Landscape**
   Pencil on paper
   27·9 × 38·1
   "Watercolours and Drawings." Arts Council. 1968/9
   "Decade. 1920 – 1930." Arts Council. 1970
   "Romanticism Continued." Arts Council. 1981
   "Experience of Landscape." South Bank Centre. 1987
   (Arts Council collection)

2. **Banks Head. Cumberland**
   1928
   Oil on canvas
   37·8 × 45.7
   "Modern Masterpieces: 20th Century British Art from the Rugby Collection."
   Cheltenham Art Gallery. 1990
   "Images of British Life." Mead Gallery, Warwick University. 1990
   (Rugby Borough Council on loan to the University of Warwick)

3. **Cumberland Landscape**
   Pencil on paper
   25·5 × 35·5
   [ex J. Ede]
   (Scottish National Gallery of Modern Art)

4. **Irthing Valley**
   1928
   Pencil on paper
   27·9 × 38·1
   (Private collection)

5. **Self Portrait**
   1927
   Oil on canvas
   129·5 × 97·7
   (Kettle's Yard, University of Cambridge)

6. **Cumberland Landscape**
   1928
   Oil on canvas
   50·8 × 60·9
   "Christopher Wood. Exhibition of Complete Works." New Burlington Galleries, London. 1938
   "A Selection from the Rutherston Collection. Oil Paintings." Arts Council. 1947/8
   "Christopher Wood." Graves Art Gallery, Sheffield. 1977
   "Christopher Wood." Arts Council. 1979
   "Christopher Wood, The Last Years." Newlyn Orion, Cornwall. 1989/90
   (Manchester City Art Galleries)

7. **Winter Landscape, Cumberland**
   1928
   Pencil on paper
   30·5 × 43·2
   "Summer Show." Redfern Gallery, London. 1945.
   (Collection of Alberto de Lacerda)

WINIFRED NICHOLSON

8. **Irthing Snow**
   Oil on board
   53·3 × 71·1
   "A Tribute to Winifred Nicholson". Abbot Hall Art Gallery, Cumbria. 1982
   (Mr and Mrs Andras Kalman)

9. **Large Landscape with Two Houses (Landscape: Road along the Roman Wall)**
   Oil on canvas
   127 × 190
   (Kettle's Yard, University of Cambridge)

10. **The Swaites**
    1923
    Oil on canvas
    56 × 76
    "Winifred Nicholson." Tate Gallery, London. 1987
    (Private collection)

11. **Northrigg Hill**
    Oil on canvas
    48·9 × 89·5
    (Private collection)

12. **Fire and Water**
    1927
    Oil on canvas
    68·5 × 55·8
    (Private collection)

13. **Amy in the Kitchen at Banks Head**
    1929
    Oil on canvas
    60·9 × 55·8
    (Private collection)

    N.B. This canvas is painted on the reverse with a portrait in oils of Vera Moore, which is
    thought to be a study from life for the portrait of the pianist reproduced in *Unknown Colour*
    (Faber and Faber. 1987. p 237.)

14. **Banks Head Flowers in an Alabaster Vase**
    Oil on canvas
    54 × 65
    (Private collection)

15. **Flower in a Brown Jar**
    1930
    Oil on canvas
    74 × 58
    XIXth Biennial International Art Exhibition, Venice. 1934
    (Private collection)

BEN NICHOLSON

16. A wooden model of a traditionally built Cumberland stone cottage
    Shaped wood, painted in oils
    30 × 12 (× 12 deep)
    (Private collection)

17. **Window at Banks Head**
    Pencil on paper
    22·8 × 30·4
    (Fine Art Society)

18. **Birch Craig Winter**
    1930
    Oil on canvas
    61 × 92
    "Ben Nicholson." Tate Gallery, London. 1969
    (Private collection)

19. **Birch Craig Summer**
    Oil on canvas
    51 × 61
    (Private collection)

20. **Walton Wood Cottage No.1**
    1928
    Oil on canvas
    56 × 61
    Lefevre Gallery, London. 1928
    "Ben Nicholson." Tate Gallery, London. 1969
    [ex Helen Sutherland]
    (Scottish National Gallery of Modern Art)

21. **Cumberland Landscape**
    Pencil on paper
    34·5 × 43
    [ex Helen Sutherland]
    (Private collection)

22. **Hare Hill**
    1930
    Oil on canvas
    54 × 69
    [ex Helen Sutherland]
    (Private collection)

23. **Landscape with Haystacks**
    1928
    Oil on canvas
    51·5 × 57
    [ex Helen Sutherland]
    "The Helen Sutherland Collection." Arts Council. 1970/71
    (Private collection)

24. **Striped Jug and Flowers**
    1928
    Oil on canvas
    39 × 38
    (Private collection)

25. **Banks Head Studio, Looking East**
    Oil on canvas
    51 × 76
    Laing Art Gallery, Newcastle upon Tyne. 1959
    Kunsthall, Bern. 1961
    Albright Knox, Buffalo. USA. 1978
    Kettles Yard, Cambridge. 1983
    (Private collection)

26. **Kingwater Valley**
    Oil on canvas
    57 × 68.5
    Kunsthall, Bern. 1961
    (Private collection)

IVON HITCHENS

27. **Cottage Bedroom**
    1925
    Oil on canvas
    60·9 × 50·8
    "One Man Show." Mayor Galleries, London. 1925
    (Private collection)

28. **The Window Sill**
    1925
    Oil on canvas
    60·9 × 50·8
    "One Man Show." Mayor Galleries, London. 1925
    (Private collection)

29. **The Bridge at Lanercost**
    Watercolour and pencil on paper
    26·6 × 38·1
    "The Viewfinders Exhibition." Abbot Hall Art Gallery, Cumbria. 1980
    (Lake District Art Gallery & Museum Trust)

30. **Abstract Interior**
    1925
    Oil on canvas
    60·9 × 50·8
    "One Man Show." Mayor Galleries, London. 1925
    "Daily Express Young Artists Exhibition." 1925
    (Ivor Braka)

31. **The Green Table**
    1925
    Oil on canvas
    60·9 × 50·8
    "One Man Show." Mayor Galleries, London 1925
    (Private collection)

32. **Cottage Interior**
    1925
    Oil on canvas
    60·9 × 50·8
    "One Man Show." Mayor Galleries, London. 1925
    (Private collection)

PAUL NASH

33. **The Walnut Tree**
    1924
    Pencil and crayon on paper
    30·5 × 23·5
    (Piccadilly Gallery)

34. **Trees and Cottages, Cumberland**
    1924
    Pencil and crayon on paper
    22·8 × 30·4
    (Board of Trustees of the Victoria and Albert Museum)

Exhibition Dates

Tullie House 17.8.91 – 25.9.91
(Carlisle)

Kettle's Yard 5.10.91 – 30.11.91
(Cambridge)

York City Art Gallery 14.12.91 – 26.1.92

Pallant House 7.2.92 – 30.3.92
(Chichester)

Abbot Hall Art Gallery 10.4.92 – 12.6.92
(Kendal)